Singing from the Darktime

SINGING FROM THE DARKTIME

A Childhood Memoir in Poetry and Prose

S. Weilbach

McGill-Queen's University Press
Montreal & Kingston · London · Ithaca

© McGill-Queen's University Press 2011
ISBN 978-0-7735-3864-1

Legal deposit first quarter 2011
Bibliothèque nationale du Québec

Printed in Canada on acid-free paper that is 100% ancient forest free (100%
post-consumer recycled), processed chlorine free

McGill-Queen's University Press acknowledges the support of the Canada
Council for the Arts for our publishing program. We also acknowledge the financial
support of the Government of Canada through the Canada Book Fund for our
publishing activities.

Library and Archives Canada Cataloguing in Publication

Weilbach, S.
Singing from the darktime : a childhood memoir in poetry and prose /
S. Weilbach.

Includes bibliographical references.
ISBN 978-0-7735-3864-1

1. Weilbach, S. – Childhood and youth – Poetry. 2. Jews – Germany –
Biography. 3. World War, 1939–1945 – Jews – Poetry. 4. St. Louis (Ship) –
Poetry. 5. Jewish refugees – England – Poetry. I. Title.

PS8645.E44S55 2011   C811'.6   C2010-907745-8

Set in 12/14.6 Mrs Eaves
Book design & typesetting by Garet Markvoort, zijn digital

For Oma

Contents

Preface   ix

Acknowledgments   xi

Preface

Over the years I've cautiously been asked to speak about my life as a very young child in Nazi Germany – cautiously, with the assumption that doing so might be painful. And because this indeed is so, I've always politely refused.

But more recently, as a grandmother of small children, memories of that time, and most significantly of my own grandmother, Oma, have moved to the forefront of my consciousness. And with them has come a compelling desire to record what I still know of those years before the war, and of Oma's special presence. I've not attempted a factual account, but have tried to revive my direct, in-the-moment experiences with all their original emotional impact. (My daily meditation practice has been an invaluable aid in reliving the most disturbing of these events.)

So that the reader experiences the young narrator's private world firsthand, with no intervening explanations of the surrounding circumstances, their historical context is outlined at the end of the book, in a separate Afterword written by Doris L. Bergen.

Though I was unsure that these pages would interest readers beyond my family, the initial enthusiasm and support of several author friends encouraged me to share them with a wider audience. In doing so I hope to convey my gratitude for many acts of kindness by those remembered or never known, particularly by those Germans whose sympathy became a danger to themselves. The very existence of such people remains an ongoing cause for gratefulness.

S. Weilbach
British Columbia, 2010

Acknowledgments

I offer my most grateful thanks to Graham Good, English
professor and poet, for his initial praise and active
encouragement towards this book's publication, and to
Ann Pearson, university lecturer, for her acute insights and
ongoing support through every stage of the work. As well,
I extend heartfelt thanks to Franka Cordua-von Specht,
journalist, for her perceptive reading and Internet research
support; to my childhood neighbour and lifelong friend, Ilse
Speck, for her help in confirming my long-ago memories of
our shared village surroundings; and to the Buddhist teacher
Kristin Penn, for her enthusiasm and practical assistance with
this project.

I'm most grateful, also, to the press's editor, Mark Abley,
for his keen judgment and invaluable guidance through every

step of the publishing process. And, finally, my loving thanks go to the daughter whose deep questions led me to embark on this work.

Singing from the Darktime

~)

The bird that sings in the morning, you'd warned …

I

In Oma's House

And was each pin I'd held
For the coil at the nape of your neck,
My Oma,
Seized for the Führer's use,
As you stood naked, trembling, praying
(if you still could pray, beloved Oma)
In a line of naked strangers
On your way to the gas-shower door?

Der Vogel der Morgens singt
Wird Abends bei der Katze gefressen.
The bird that sings in the mornings
Shall be devoured by the cat at night.

Opa, who shares your wide bed,
His sweeping white moustache
A guileless mirror of von Hindenburg's –
(vain talisman, perhaps,
against our unsuspected fates) –
Who rose at dawn and now

Eyes how the cowman's rhythmic fork
Lifts, swings, drops manure
Onto the mound along the stable wall.
Lifts, swings, tips, silent, not whistling
While Opa's here.
His eyes below the visor of his cap
Avoiding Opa's face.
For how long now has he not met his gaze?

Beside his kennel our yard-dog shifts.
His chain drags harsh on unrepaired cement.
Without a glance towards its scrape
(this beast I pity and I fear)
Opa goes through the stable door
To watch my father rattle milk
Into the empty singing pail.
One restless beast swings round her head
And Opa slaps a greeting on her rump.
"Good morning, Father," says his son
Against his cow's broad flank.
From further down another lows.
Then, "Milk her next!" Opa commands.
With fingers deft and long

My father draws the milk
From pink and wrinkled teats.

The cowman done, thrusts shovel hard
Into the steaming, reeking mound,
Clops to the iron pump in wooden clogs,
Bends to catch water in his open mouth.
Then runs it over outstretched hands.
And Opa calls, "Albert! The soap."
And still their eyes do not connect.
And Albert settles on a stool
To fill another pail with milk.

Then Opa lifts a brimful one,
Steps cautiously in third-best shoes,
Past cow shit, past manure stench,
Across the early morning yard
Toward our open farmhouse door.
Scours shoes across the scraper-blade,
Steps briskly in.
Rubs soles and sides across the mat,
And brings into our kitchen
Faint lingerings of the barn.

I sip my milky cocoa
To the bottom of my cup,
Breathe in the pail's warm, frothing milk.
A silent, avid watcher
At this daily morning dance.

And you, my Oma, nod your thanks,
While mother, plump and small
In sky-blue, eye-blue apron,
Rings gold, sliced-open plums
Around and round and round again
Onto a soft and moon-faced dough.

Now from the room beyond
I hear his paper rustle,
Then Opa makes it snap.
Then all again is quiet.
Grey light comes sliding through
From narrow shrouded windows,
Where a passage to the field
No wider than a cow,
Is only bright at noon.

When sunlight falls between us
And the grey-walled house next door.

The flat stone basin,
Sidehole bunged tight
With a large and squeaking cork,
Sits ready, cold and wide upon the tabletop,
For Oma's tipped-in pail of flowing white.
It settles warm and still,
Until I help to let it flow
From sidehole into shining cans.
Its velvet cream clings thick and fat
Against the basin's empty walls.
And I will have a chunk of moist black bread
To wipe the sweet and buttery stuff
Into my small and eager mouth.

A clack, clack-clack comes clattering
From the alleyway.
One beast, another, and another,
Hoofs clicking
On cobble and on stone

Like iron-wheeled freights
On iron railway tracks.

And Oma, did you hear
On your Auschwitz-going train,
Our milk-cows clattering
For one last time
On their morning meadow way?
Brush, swish, through green long grass,
Munching, chewing, stopped in sunlight,
Knee-high in dandelions, in poppies,
In cornflowers beside the quick, clean stream?

Albert drives them there
To feed, to drowse,
Or stumble down and curl their tongues
Round the clear, cool, swift brook,
Rippling, streaming on sunlit, pebbled sand.
While whistling past the kitchen window,
His curved stick knocks
An idle rhythm
Against the kitchen wall.

Our last unbroken year.

Oma's my air, the water I drink,
The breads I eat: white, brown, black.
I touch their naked, unbaked flesh,
Alive and slowly rising.
Their wheat-yeast smell trapped
In lightwashed linen,
Signed with your name, my Oma,
In fine white threads
Stitched by your dreaming maiden hands.

Outside: the golden scent of ripening plums,
A searching hum of worker bees,
Cat's silky windings at my legs.
I perch beside you on the steps
And learn to count the jade jewel beads
That seem to leap out from their pods
With a pea-sweet taste of spring …
And not of winters past or those to come.

The pea bowl full, you send a silent smile
For me to follow you
From task to task.
To hold a wooden spoon,
To stir, to sip,
To find your misplaced spectacles.
To take a dish of milk
To the sharptoothed, fearsome dog.

Beyond our iron gates
The silent village street,
With clean-washed cobbles.
A tiny gutter stream
Where I can float a twig,
My mother's little hollowed gourd,
A folded paper boat that sinks.

The air is always still before and after
Cattle's sudden clatter, horsecart's iron wheels.
At night there is no street, no world
Beyond our fastened gate,
Our heavy wooden window shutters.
Perhaps I only dreamed

I held my father's hand
And walked in glaring moonlight,
Cobble shadows sharp and deep,
To the street's far end,
Where voices rumbled back and forth
Above my ears.
And my almost-sleeping arm
Danced moonshadows black and long
Across the silver ground.

Morning gleams white, narrow bars of light
Upon the wall beyond my bed,
Till mother spreads the shutters wide
And hooks them fast against the wall.
The coming day holds all
My dearest knowns,
Perhaps with one swift sweet surprise
When Opa from some glittering distant source
Hands me a little golden netted bag
Packed tight with shining chocolate coins.

Or Marta with the yellow braids
Will come across the yard

And on our slippery flagstone floor
We build a snaking, twisting train
With black-white wooden dominoes.
Or with imaginary flames
Brew dollpots full of cherry tea,
Or coffee ground from farmyard stones.

Until the day she leaves for school
And comes no more.
Except just once to teach me
What she's learned
And I do not yet know:
That I and mine are loathsome Jews.
That she and hers, respected Folk,
No longer shall consort with us.

(And Oma, did you ever know
what I had never told,
but held in deepest shame
beside my childish fears?
That my first day in school
was not the joy you'd thought?

That I was made to shrink
upon the hindmost, darkest bench
amongst the gypsy boys,
where teacher proclaimed all shall sit
who stink and foul
the Führer's pristine air?)

From then on down the years
I saw yet could not grasp,
There's beauty that comes linked with pain,
And cruelty's often side-by-side
With joy in someone's heart.
How strange it seemed that
Passing on the street
The people warmly said, *Grüss Gott*
And Oma called him *Lieber Gott*,
And whispered, *Gott sei Dank*
When she gave thanks
Or breathed a wishful prayer.

As if this god were good and kind.
Though he saw every thought and deed

Without one heavenly finger raised
To warn, or stop, or punish
Those who maimed and harmed.

How lonely I became
Once I was shown this heedless Power
Who on some lofty throne
Stayed mute and still
When someone tore the wings off flies
Or struck a helpless beast.
When all your prayerful pleas, my Oma,
Still would not end such wrongs,
I turned and gave my heart
To simple, gentle things.
Like cows and spotted ladybirds,
Like streams and flowers,
And flapping storks
Ascending from our pointed roofs.
(For whom I set out sugar cubes
to bring a longed-for second child.)

Atop our washed and bundled sheets
I rode the washerwoman's cart
Through iron gate, past passage walls,
Past bushes thick with twittering birds,
Until we reached the grey, flat stone
Beside the racing stream.
Where then she rinsed and flung and wrung,
Then let one last piece float –
A billowing white balloon –
So I would laugh again
When I had cried about a bleeding knee.

Then I had dipped my hand
Into this sparkling waterworld,
But quickly pulled it out
When curly strings
Of bright red river-worms slid near
To suck and draw my blood.

Once in that green-scented field
With scattered saplings – oaks and elms –
I saw a shining russet bead

Inside a deepgreen leaf –
A gall provoked by mold or wasps,
As pretty as my mother's silver brooch.

And once, while dawdling in the grass,
I caught a glimpse of Opa,
With jaunty stride and swinging cane
Move down a path towards the train.
Until he paused
And bending deftly to one side
Blew snot upon the ground.
Then wiped his finger in the grass
And strode away,
His clean silk handkerchief
Still pointing from the pocket of his suit
Beside the glossy tie, the goldpearled pin.

This pin he wore, as well,
To lead the other men
In prayers and in song.
His notes made clear and pure,
He said, by swallowed uncooked yolks
Just taken from a heedless hen.

And though at six I was too small
To understand his words,
I caught the fret and worry
In his tone, that for a long time now
There had not been ten youths or men
With whom to worship
In our Hebrew house of God.

The synagogue was down the cobbled street,
To which we walked
In our fresh Sabbath clothes.
My stockings white and drawn up tight,
My little shiny shoes like new,
Untouched by weekday's farmyard dung,
Or pasture mud and sand.
And mother had small garnets in her ears,
A tiny diamond on her hand.
And father combed his curls down flat.
And my dear Oma had
A slender shining feather
Sewn slanting on her wide-brimmed hat,
And gold-pinned lace so lovely at her neck.

But when we climbed the worn familiar stair
Towards our women-places in the gallery,
We found ourselves alone
Above the nearly empty hall,
Above the lonely, full-voiced chants
Before the darkwood case
That housed the velvet-covered scroll.
And while these last few men
Intoned their tuneful prayers
And our two mothers joined their song,
I held my tongue
Though I had learned the words.
And with my small, clean handkerchief
Formed dolls and cats
And crowns and birds –
My secret pagan offerings
To that fair-minded unknown deity
Who'd cause the teacher in the school
To cower or run or slink away,
Just like the villain in a fairytale.
Or Max and Moritz,
Cruel and vicious boys,
For penance turned to ice,

Then melted into unmourned urns –
Their family's empty pickle jars.

And as I held my Oma's
And my mother's lacegloved hands,
We'd hurry home before the men,
And guarded thus
I did not need to fear
The bands of stretchnecked, hissing geese
That often barred the street.
Nor sly, malicious, brutal girls
Who silent watched me
Make my way to school,
Then hurled a chain of sharp-edged stones
Against my back
Along with spiteful names.

But later, all at home again,
We'd sing the grace, and dine
On heavenly things made not by God,
But by my Oma's and my mother's hands.
First, soups or broths, then meats or carp
In sauces sharp or sweet.

Young carrots, peas, fresh salads soft and mild,
And at the end a slice of torte
Or cake. Perhaps a sponge soaked deep
In frothy eggs and wine,
A *Traubentorte* with green and perfect grapes,
Plucked from a friendly neighbour's vine.
Or nutcake made with hazels
Ground as rich and fine as flour,
And with a glossy, darkbrown chocolate cloak
That spread a kind of wordless poetry
On my expectant tongue.

These are the joys of Oma's house,
Where in the stable I can watch
The cowman squirt
A long straight stream of milk
Into the barncat's widestretched mouth.
Or sometimes as a sudden treat
Be lifted to a cow's wide back
To laugh and cling
With head laid close against the strong warm neck.

When going to my other Oma's house
We make what seems a journey of a thousand hours.
There is a hot and sooty smell,
The train's white gasps of pluming steam.
Inside are seats of yellow wood
And roughly rattling windowpanes.
My mother frowns to see me kneel,
To rest my face
Against the grimy glass,
And gaze at passing streams and farms.
For now my snowy stockings
Will be grey.
And she will have to grasp my chin,
To hold me still
And scrub my smutty, smarting cheeks,
To work away the greasy streaks
With spit-wet corners of her handkerchief.

On the lonely evening platform
There's other Oma's bristly kiss,
And other Opa's smiling pat upon my head.
His round, unseeing eyes
Gaze somewhere far away,

At something only he can see.
Their voices greet with Hessen's rolling r's.
Then we four walk the narrow, cobbled streets
To a house where treats are not
Alluring food, or fields and beasts,
But bedtime rhymes of paradox:
Die Nacht war Schwartz
Der Mond schien helle
Wenn auf der Sandbank blitzeschnelle
Langsam ein Hase fuhr Schlittschuh ....
And deeply thrilling fairy tales
With fearsome forests dense and dark
Or children gone astray with bitter, frozen hearts.
But also learning how to weave.
To make a snaking, coloured cord
Slide through an empty cotton reel
Like toothpaste from a tube.

A warm but silent house
Whose Opa sits and prays
For hours on end.
And winds a prayer-thong
Round and round his arm

To crown it with a leather cube –
A sealed and holy little vault,
For his revered and fabled King.

The rooms are full of Him.
An irate vengeful god,
Who shot a knife of lightning
And snarling thunder-shouts
Into the very room
Where at first light
I broke a Sabbath rule,
And with my tempted hands
Made a forbidden tear
Through papers sealed
Around a waiting birthday toy.
And instant vengeance came
From that exacting Power
Who hovered through this house.
Unlike the distant Being
To whom my other Oma spoke.

On our return
I stroked the docile cows,

Brought cooked potatoes to the dog
Who looked less fearsome now.
Let Opa hold me on his knee,
And found it droll
When Oma stuck her glasses in her hair
To see a tiny needlehole
And fill it with a pointed thread.

And later on that night,
Inside my linen sheets,
I thought how in that other house
God's lightning came –
A fearful, blinding flash,
While here,
Though punishments did sting
My body and my pride
(A hard slap on the cheek for
a rebellious word
or in the lonely corner
standing still and dark
with face towards the wall)
They were not meant to seize
My private, inmost soul.

(That soul *was* harmed
when in the village school
each day I had to raise my arm
to say *Heil Hitler* with the rest.)

On summer nights
So that they would not harm me
With their savage probes,
My father chased mosquitoes
From my darkening room
Or flattened them upon the walls.
Faint, tiny scribbles,
With a fatal smudge of pink,
Until the snowy net was draped
And tented round my bed.
And then I'd hear the voices
From below the stairs.
The muted rattling of a pail, a laugh,
And uncle's jovial song
Sung loud so I would hear:
Meine Oma fährt Motorad

Ohne Bremse, ohne Licht,
Und der Schupo an der Ecke
Sie spuckt Ihm ins Gesicht.
But then I'd shed some trickling tears
Because I was alone,
While they might joke
Or sing a song,
Then say things strange to hear.
How this one's left,
And that one's gone
Though no one knows to where.
And how they'd take our cows.
And words I'd never heard before
Like Uruguay, or Ecuador, or Montevideo.
And was it now too late?

But then first light would come,
The shutters wide again,
My curtains rippling in the air
With early farmyard sounds,
Or some romantic melody
From our downstairs radio.
And thumps and thuds

Of breaddough under Oma's hands.
Or it might be an autumn day ...
Was it the last?
When I lay hot and ill
With coughs and whoops and gasps,
Until my mother's healing teas
Of camomile and mint
Would bring a moment's peace.
Or Oma's creamy goosefat salve
Would spread a soothing warmth
Across my aching, heaving chest.

And then I would be well again
With winter past and gone to spring.
When there'd be gooseberries for jam,
And Mirabellen plums
Locked tight in gleaming jars
Deep in our house's lightless bowels.
Where I knew fearsome spiders lurked,
All dark and large as mice,
Each waiting for a strike.
Each baleful cousin
To the monstrous beast

Perched like a threatening *Hakenkreutz*
Upon the porcelain toilet bowl,
Where I would cry and scream
If I were made to go.

But if I'd cried until my throat was raw
There might be someone
With a cool, pink glass
Of sweet and subtle *Himbeersaft.*
My papa, or the uncle from America
Who made me laugh
And rode me on his back,
And pranced and danced,
And taught me how to sing,
"O du lieber Augustin,
Augustin, Augustin,
O du lieber Augustin,
Alles ist hin!"

＝)

At that last winter's dusk
A girl tapped on our door,

A silver crown upon her golden head.
Her dress and boots were sparkling white.
She held a basket on one arm
With little gifts and cakes,
A gingerbread St. Niklaus
Poised ready in one hand.
But when she saw me at the door
Her hand flew to her mouth.
As if she'd done some dreadful wrong
She fled back down the steps,
And as she ran declared,
The Christchild had no gift
To give the likes of us.

I did not mind about the cake,
But these few callous words
Plunged deep into my heart.
Because I'd found her
Lovely to behold
They caused a wound both long and deep.

One morning on my solitary way
Towards the dreaded school,
There was a noise we almost never heard –
The roaring of a rapid truck.
It drove right past
And vanished round a bend.

Then as I sat
To learn to spell a word,
At Teacher's sudden call
The class erupted from their seats,
And clustering at the sill,
Looked down upon the yard
And grinned or laughed.
We in the back
Were told to rise and look.
I barely knew then what I saw –
It was so strange
It would not fit into my mind:
A circle like a children's game
Of fullgrown men
I'd never seen before.

They circled in the cobbled yard
Around and round and round again.
While at the side two men in uniform
Looked on and smiled.
Until an old man stumbled
And a swift, swastikaed arm
Dragged him apart.
Then he was kneed until he almost fell
And pushed to where I could not see.

And in that silent troupe
Treading round and round and round again,
I thought I saw my father walk
With all those other men.

When I came home
Our house was quiet,
But for my mother's rapid steps
Upstairs from room to room.
(Where no one went this time of day.)
And when I ran
With satchel bouncing at my back

To meet my Oma at the stove,
Or find her seated on the couch,
She was not there.
Nor Opa anywhere.
And when I ran into the yard
Where I heard anxious lowing calls
From restless cows within their stalls,
There were two men
Forcing them out with sticks and shouts
To jostle on the cobbled street.
Where lowing and clattering
In affrighted haste
I saw them trot away.

And then succeeded
Eerie silent hours,
Or was it days?
My shocked mind could not tell.
As mother cooked and moved so fast
I did not dare the chance to ask
The frightened questions
Hovering at the edge of thought.

Then I went into Oma's room
And climbed onto the bed
And on her pillow
Smelled the faintest trace
Of lavender and baking bread.
And found a wavy silver hair
Caught in the heavy comb
Left on the lace-edged sheet.

Though with its clean familiar stink
Of straw and dung
And cows in milk,
The stable now was bare of life.
No fitful hoof scuffed on the floor,
No placid munching at the hay.
The yard dog, too, was gone.
I stared and stood
In frozen quiet
Until my mother came
And pulled me back inside the house.
And thrust the heavy doorbolt tight.
And then in each and every room

Closed every shutter,
Long before the night.

That night I lay in mother's bed
Where father always slept.
And from the black and silent street
Glared weird and awful streaks of light,
Through the closed shutters' vents.
Their cryptic warnings slid across our walls.
I barely slept
While mother moved about the house.

But once I dreamt a dreadful dream.
Hänsel and Gretel's forest
Stretched all dense and dark
To the farthest ends of earth.
And no bird flew or sang.
And in her apron
Oma wandered all alone
With nothing in her hands.
I was afraid,
Yet still in blessed ignorance

With every anxious breath
Drew in the comfort
Of my parents' bed.
And tried to think of happy ways
My scary fairytale could end.

2

Devoured at Night

A battering storm, a gale,
A hundred thunderous hammers pound
Their metal-shattering strikes
Against the bolted wooden door.
Its sagging bottom shrieks
Across the limestone floor.
The shutters slam back wide.
And smashing window-glass
Rings like a splitting bell.
Its swords and spikes descend.
The morning light floods in
As any other day.

My throat's locked tight.
No breath, no beat of heart.
My back pressed close against the wall.
My mother's back is inches from my eyes.
From somewhere far comes Marta's scream.
She falls into the well.
My throat's locked tight.

Its wings on fire
A stork flaps in a mist of smoke.

Their steps move swift and near.
A rusty axe-blade breaks
A cut-glass bottle in its pink silk web.
My mother's mirror cracks.
A swelling sharp-sweet scent
Is pungent in my mouth.
They thud upon the stairs.
My mother pins me to the wall.
I cling onto her clammy hand.

The cows are bellowing loud and long
Although they're gone.

A bulky shape hurls past
A shattered windowpane.
It thumps and clatters in the yard.
The attic thunders loud with wrath.

My mother drags me down the stairs
And grabs a jacket from the wall.
My slippers loose upon my feet
I trip and stumble as we run.
There's many crowding in our yard.

They stoop and crouch to search
Among the broken scatterings.
There's Marta's father, too.
And as we flee he speaks
To mother quick and low,
His eyes afraid and kind.

⁊

The little boy with wide grey eyes
And knee socks brilliant white,
Stares up at me
From where he pulls
A toytrain engine on a silver track.
They say I'm in an auntie's house.
The air is stale and cool.
There is no warm and crackling stove.

Beyond the window
Tramcars clang and rumble by,
And chimney fingers
Point up to the clouds.

The boy wants me
To play with him.
I hold the traintrack down
While back and forth he slides
The bright green engine
With its tinkling golden bell.

I think of my pink doll,
The one that Opa bought,
With little lashes at her eyes,
The tiny skirt my Oma sewed.
I saw her plunging to the ground.
But mother would not let me stop
To bend and pick her up.

I cease to hold the traintrack down
And climb onto the folding cot
Where later I must sleep.
With prudent care
The boy removes the gleaming train,
And from a drawer at the wall
He brings a book,
And asks if I will read to him

Before he goes to bed.
Although I cannot read its words
I see a picture that I know.
A wolf with many pointed teeth
Sits grinning wickedly
Upon a snowy bed.
A ruffled granny-cap's
Perched slyly on his ears.
I do not tell I can't yet read,
Instead begin the tale:

There is the wood,
Its presence sinister and black.
There are the children
Wandering.
Hungry, and afraid,
Now very far from home.

But then the story
Takes an unexpected turn:
They come upon
A vast and blazing fire
And feel its dreadful heat.

While from the trees around
Fly games and dolls
And hoops and balls
To perish in the flames.
And wildly shouting men
Come running from the night,
With menace in their reaching hands
All tipped with curving metal claws.

I crook my fingers into hooks
To show just what I mean.
At once the small boy shrinks away,
His eyes are round with fear.
But still I cannot stop.
A newborn devil in my heart
Is angry at his city clothes,
His unread stack of coloured books,
His milkwhite innocence.
I tell him how the little boy
Is chased still deeper in the trees.
And when I do
He turns away
With hands pressed to his ears.

And I am guilty and ashamed.

And was I there for hours,
Or days or weeks or months?
My mother was not there to ask,
Though she was meant to come
When all her urgent crucial things
Had finally been done.

I saw the dusk come on the street.
Within a light was on.
I ate a sparse and tasteless meal
Set on the polished tablewood
With fancy rounds of lace.
I heard a housebell shrill beyond the door.
And someone jerked me from my chair
And whisperhissed against my ear
That I must, silent as a mouse,
Squeeze and lie still,
And stay inside the cooped-up dark
Behind their china cupboard door.

And then there was another house
All square and wide and high.
It had so many winding stairs
I dared not gaze below
Or leave the shelter of our little room
To climb them down.
The steps were glassy grey,
And narrowed to a point
While circling down in dizzying descent.

There was an alien thing – a lift –
With metal folding gates
That rattled up and down,
Where mother said, before she left,
She'd let me go
If I was not alone.
(As if there were a place somewhere
where I would want to go
if Oma was not there.)

An unknown neighbour took me down
To see the street and shops below.

But I was far too scared to look.
Instead of friendly village streets
Here cars dashed fast,
Enormous buses roared.
Just when they'd stopped
They once more leapt ahead.
I was quite sure they'd knock me down,
And so hung back.
And begged if I might now return
To our silent, empty room.
Where, if my will and wish were fierce enough
I thought I somehow might restore and mend
All that was gone.

Those times when hunger struck
I fed on meals my memory prepared:
Red cabbage with its sweet-sour tang,
And forks of crumbling chestnut meats
With goldbrown bites of roasted goose.
Or I would pine for something sweet,
Like dumplings ovenbaked
And resting in a creamy sauce of caramel.

This made me long for Oma's face
Bent to the stove with utmost care
To stir her sauce all glossy smooth
Without a single lump or scorch.
I tried to call her to my side
From that long nowhere
Where she'd gone
And could not think where it might be.

I did not trust what mother said:
That they were with an aunt.
For if they were, my Oma
Would have cleaned and packed her comb,
And kissed me well before they'd gone.
And Opa would have pinched my cheek
And asked me what I'd like
On their return.

Though mother did not say
Where father was,
I'd heard it whispered
He was locked away
By those swastikaed men,

Who'd let him out for golden cash
Which mother went alone each day to find.
I knew not where.

Suspended in this vacant realm
I tried to soothe myself
With tales I'd heard
From Oma of the bristly chin.
But made myself afraid. And wept.

Such a journey on a train at night
We'd never made before,
With people huddled everywhere
Asleep, curled on the floor,
Or pressed in silent swaying ranks
In every passageway.
They looked like spectres to my eyes
With faces tinted blue
By one bulb's feeble light.
I dozed on mother's lap.

When I first saw that gaunt and distant man
I shrank away.
He did not greet me with a smile
Or speak my name.
His height was bent,
His scalp was naked and his fingers shook.
It was not he but mother
Knew the way to go
Into a ship's large, shadowy place
Where we were now to live.
My father then, and all the other silent men,
Were told to go to yet another room,
And I was glad
I did not have to look at him.

And just before they turned to go,
There came a thunderous rattling noise
Above our heads.
As if this were some phantom ship
Blown right back to our house
Where in the attic
Then and now and evermore

The axemen battered, smashed and tore.
But when a steady throbbing came
From just beneath my feet –
The heartbeat of this crowded place –
I heard my mother thank her god
That we were safe.

And then I forced myself
To look in father's face,
To ask those burning questions
I'd heard no one speak.

But father would not look at me.
He turned away to go.
His frozen silence told me
That my dreadful dream was true,
And Oma was now lost to me.

And often I have seen her
Stand and sway on feeble legs,

When once she'd stood so strong,
Her anguished mind alive with fears
Not for herself,
But for each small and grownup child
Who'd gone she knew not where.
To where she'd never know.

I long to trust
There would have passed
Through her tormented thoughts,
As she stood waiting at that final door,
Unbidden images of times gone by
As if by magic they were now:
Of Opa striding with his gallant cane;
Of perfect handmade cheeses she had formed;
And that bright day a van came to the house,
Filled with the things she'd yearned for
More than twenty years:
The gleaming table,
Long enough for twelve;
The sofa and the many chairs
With seats of blue and slippery silk.
The wandering beggar seated here,

To whom she served a rich and lavish meal,
And thanked him for his presence every year.

∾

Now from my twenty thousand days
Across unbounded space and change,
Lest I would lose my sanity
I must believe, my Oma,
That on your hard, hard, lonely way,
Some hidden nameless source
Imbued you with a full and deep repose,
An impervious, subtle shell of light
Round each last breath and thought.

3

The Boat that Did Not Sink

St. Louis of Toulouse (1274–1297), son of Charles of Anjou:
At a young age he became a member of the Franciscan mendicant
order, and a year before his early death was made a bishop. He had
a deep commitment to acts of mercy and service to the poor.
He brought food to those with leprosy; as a bishop, each day
he invited numbers of the poor to share his meals at the castle,
and gave away most of his salary.

He was canonized in 1317.

The St. Louis. How I came to this iron
Whippedcream ship of flight,
This weird receptacle of dancing and despair,
I never knew.
(Soothing and terrible not to know.)

Grey trains, long sooty nights,
Stale water in a metal cup.
The gaunt, now silent man
Who once had been my father.
The smiling sightless stare of other Opa,
And mother gone away and back,
On hidden errands, swift
As an errant pebble from a catapult
Unguided now by Oma's temperate hand.

No ready memory-hooks
For labyrinthian passageways,
For oily, dense new-painted air.
Or stippled iron steps
That clang beneath a heavy tread.

My spellbound eyes take in
Mesmeric shifting seas,
The bubbling, churning greywhite wake
Unravelling us from all there was
And all there might have been.

If down below I turn my head
In search of our own cabin door
Among the hundreds side-by-side
Along the countless passages
Without a single ray of nature's light,
Just little bulbs inside each metal cage,
For all I know
Someone will soon come floating ceiling-high,
No stranger than the thousand faces,
Voices all around,
The nameless woman with the bright pink powdery cheeks,
Who lifts my chin and asks my name
In a false and honeyed tone,
In accents never met till now.
No stranger than the shining shower
Of flying fish that flutters
On the planks at dusk.

Perhaps a witchy source of gold,
The same that set my father free?

Or the barely lit enormous, nearly empty room
I came to after darkness fell
When I had lost my way
Returning from a solitary toilet call.
Where music surged and danced and dimmed
And in midair a pale rectangle gleamed
With shadowed pictures swaying, going, gone.

One morning wandering to a deck,
I saw some little children
Playing in a box of sand,
With tiny painted houses, clocktower, trees, a train,
With wooden cows, a horse, a pig, a dog.
They lined them up and scored a sort of street into the sand.
And once again I heard the clattering of our cows
Departing on the cobblestones.

Then soon there is a Sabbath wine.
But here all's new: there's carpet everywhere,
St. Louis' trembling hull,

And steady rumblings underfoot.
I take my childsized taste
Of sodawater with a splash of wine,
And all at once, for one last time
See Oma's face again: lit yellowgold
Above a plaited candle's flame
Which she has struck alight
To greet the evening star.

Then this is swept away
By alien voices, sights and sounds.

The first rough waves throw everything atilt,
And passage floors rise to the walls,
Then pause, then drop before they rise again.
A sudden clutching at my throat
Spews vomit sour and foul onto the floor.
Without one thought or will or wish
I'm on my narrow rocking bed,
Where dashing darkgrey ocean floods,
Flung hard against the porthole glass,
Obliterate the day.

(In future years
I'd wish I'd vomited, as well,
each flying stone, each wounding slur,
each shrinking breath of fear of loss
trapped underneath my skin.)

And then the porthole's bright again.
The little glass upon its shelf
Stops rattling sickeningly,
And I can drink the cup of lemon tea
Brought to my bed
By a goldhaired stewardess.
Her uniform so white it stings my eyes.
Who offers one to mother too,
Still groaning in the cabin bunk above.

And when she gently shuts the door
I wonder at our transformed world,
This lurching home upon the sea,
Where sometimes stewards tease and grin
And pluck their cap from off their head
And twirl it on a finger, like a top.

Or mimic fear at little puffs of ocean wind
And beg a child to fetch a cup of soothing tea.

A place of fairytales come true.
With happenings for every day,
Where I heard very soon
There'd be a grownup costume dance.
Where every morning people holding wooden sticks
Sent shuffling blocks of wood
To slide across the deck.
Where men and women laughed.
And where each meal came
Served on silver trays,
And I grew fat on salmon mayonnaise
And roasted new potatoes
With a lingering butter taste.
Where I was offered ices every day
In polished glass and silver bowls,
With pink and green minute umbrellas
Perched on each frozen globe.
At every meal there was a cake or tart,
Or pastry I had never seen before.

A crunchy chocolate *Mohrenkopf,* or cocoa brandy balls,
Or tarts with cherries glowing under jellied juice,
And served with whipping cream
Built into swirling whorls.
All these rewards
Came with the passing of the violent northern seas.

It seemed as if with sun and dry cool air
A little happiness would also come.
For even father spoke to praise the food,
And mother sat at ease
Before a lifeboat, sheltered from the wind,
And sipping tea.
But nearer than the shifting clouds,
The everchanging swells and waves,
I felt another weather too:
Each face contained a hidden mood
Which did not fit with sunlit waves,
With costume balls and lavish foods.
One moment I'd be smiled upon,
Another I'd be sent away
With biting words and frowns.

There seemed no way to fathom
What next might bring them on.

I thought it best to keep away
And wander round the ship alone,
Protected by the railings round each deck
As if we sailed inside
A huge and windy baby crib,
Just like the one outgrown at home.
I never saw the ambient ferments, doubts and fears,
But drank their poison in.

Yet once I walked beyond my usual round
Till I could see St. Louis' funnels towering tall.
And here my eyes stopped short in fright.
There was a flag
That flapped and rippled in the wind
With a black swastika
On its bold red ground.
It was exactly what I'd seen
Worn on the brutal arm
That shoved an old man till he fell.

Where father also trod
In mute confusion's abject fear.
I wondered if my parents knew
And held it in their silence
With other dreadful things they might have seen.

(That night I dreamed a dream
that plagued me all my years:
A door locked fast against the night
breaks open with a crash of sound
and stamping, rushing feet
approach me where I lie in bed
to start in terror from my sleep.)

At last a steward said
We'd soon be nearing land,
And when I asked him what it would be like
He rolled his eyes and smiled
And said there would be fishes
Lighting up the nighttime sea like lamps,
And thunderstorms to strike our ears,
And heat such as we'd never known.

Then I heard someone laugh
As I walked past their cabin door.
And mother said we soon would
Pack and lock our biggest cabin-trunk
And get it carried down
To where it later would be brought ashore.
And sightless Opa spoke a different prayer
With syllables I'd never heard before.
And father walked and walked
Around the decks,
And only stopped to stare out at the waves.
He circled round and round
As if the village day he'd trod
Those terror-stricken helpless laps
Had set him on a pointless fear-filled course
Which he would follow all his days.

That evening when I walked about the ship
I saw a big saloon, with long green tables
Stretching wall to wall.
Where men and women seemed to play a game
With dice and little horses made of wood.
When some were pushed ahead

The people clapped.
How odd it seemed to me,
These grownups with their games.
At home they never played with toys
And were too occupied with work
Even to play with me.

A blaring trumpet shook me from my pre-dawn sleep,
To find our cabin stewardess smiling at the door.
She said to quickly dress
And come to eat our festive morning meal
For this was now our landing day.
My mother helped me tie
The shiny rosepink apron
Of my doll-like dirndl dress.
(A hasty purchase from St. Louis' shop,
where all were forced to leave
the little money they still had.)

The passageways were crammed with trunks.
Loud footsteps rang upon the metal stairs.
With soft grey daylight came the noise
Of weighty chains dropped to the lowest deck.

And brisk commands.
The ocean breeze had stopped its breath
And with each moment
Came an unfamiliar warmth,
Which quickly turned to heat.
And we were made to stand in lines
By men in different uniforms,
Who asked us questions in a different tongue.
They smiled and joked with every child, like friends.
And soon were done.
And left us in their chugging motorboat.

The hot air seemed to tremble
With relief and joy.
And someone somewhere gave a shout:
"Havana! We are safe!"
We went to wait on deck.
And here the sun burned on my head.
The dazzle in the sky, the glaring sea
Brought spots before my eyes,
Till I could barely see at all.
We waited there amongst our things,
And mother brought me to the rail

To see my aunt who'd fled here months ago –
A tiny figure far below,
Arms waving on the dock
Like all the others there.

But on our ship a sudden silence fell.
A forceful voice called a command
And all the crewmen ceased their noise
Of shifting trunks and cases on the deck.
An officer then spoke to us
To say there was a small delay
And we must wait below.
Amongst the crowd, we moved
And crammed through passageways
Back to our cabin.
Empty now, but for the pail of water
And the mop, in readiness beside the door.
And then our wait stretched into stifling hours
Without one breath of cooling air,
Until a kindly steward passed each door
To say there'd be a midday meal for us
Where we would hear when we could land.

These first hours quickly pass
But then come long and careful words
Which tell us we must wait till dusk
To leave the ship.
Our stewardess, without her uniform,
But in a pretty flowery dress,
Is frowning as she passes on the stairs.
When dusk descends, a silence waits.
We hear we are to stay another night on board.
My little toothbrush, comb, and sleeping things
Are now unpacked once more.
And in the airless, humid dark
I sense how all are now on edge
And cannot fall asleep.

The morning meal is only coffee, toast, and jam,
And served by men who do not smile
As they had smiled before.
The sun shines fiercely
On the sweltering deck
With an angry, white-hot fire.
My mother covers up my head
And wears a spotted visor from the shop.

When I look down upon the harbour's dazzling glare
I see a hundred little boats
Crowd near St. Louis' hull.
My aunt and uncle small as dolls
Stare up from one, and open wide their mouths to call.
But are too faint to clearly hear.
Then they are rowed ashore
From where they wave and wave
Until they're made to go away.

As people crowd into an empty large saloon
I hear a voice call out and beg for calm.
And someone bends to say to me
That I must go and play on deck,
For this is grownup business now.

Up on the deck a steward
Has unlocked a game of shuffleboard
To let some older children play.
He beckons me to come as well.
But now my eyes ache in the glaring light,
My throat sticks dry as dust, although
The heat clings damp to every inch of skin.

Before I turn away, I see
The little boats are coming back again.

The deck they call the Promenade
Is partly shaded here.
It has glass walls against the gales,
But Cuba sends no moving air
To ruffle through my hair and cool my face.
The empty deckchairs line along the painted wall,
And I sit down and watch the seabirds swoop.
But all at once I hear some footsteps race
Across the boards above my head
And someone yelling, "No-o-o-o!"
When I stand up to look
A sudden bright red streak
Is trickling down the glassy wall.
From every side the people run.
A woman in a purple dressing-gown
Bursts through the bulkhead door
Near where I stand.
She screams and screams.

A big girl who befriended me one day at sea
Is pulling at my arm to make me move away.
I ask her what she knows, what she has seen.
She whispers very low a dark and terrifying word:
Selbstmord, and brings me
To the sport-deck's swimming pool
To see some children learning how to float.
And very soon my mother comes in search of me.
She reprimands me angrily – for what I am not sure –
And takes me to our cabin
Where I must wait in isolated banishment.
Here from the open porthole I can see
How all the little rowing-boats
Are heading quickly for the shore.
And from some faroff place upon our ship
I hear the ringing of a calling bell,
And then the feet of people
Hurrying past our cabin door.

There follow hours, then days
Of scorching, penetrating heat.

And sometimes crashing, thunderous rains
Come down, then quickly stop again.
And every morning from the shore
The rowboats with their hailing passengers
Rock close beside St. Louis' hull.
I see my aunt gaze up at us
But she no longer waves.
And once she tries and fails to fling
A letter to our deck.
It ends up floating on the sea.
And father frowns and mutters to himself
And frets whose letter it had been.

Despite the blazing sky,
Their busy clamour as the shorebirds flap and fly,
We are as if becalmed in deep and suffocating fog.
I see each grownup face set grim,
Or marked with blatant fear.
The stewards in the dining-room no longer grin,
Nor are there chocolate ices any more.
The big girl who befriended me
Now tells me other things to know:

About committees, meetings and appeals for help
To save us from that dreadful place
Where both our fathers would have died.
She says if here we cannot land
Then that is where we'll have to go.

Now from Havana's dock
They're loading countless crates and sacks.
And when my parents say they do not know,
I ask a steward why.
He quickly looks around,
Then pats me on my head
And says, "I cannot say."
And at that kindly touch
My frozen feelings thaw.
I turn away to hide
The heartsick frightened stored-up tears
Now suddenly released.

Now sightless Opa
Never stops his whispered prayers.
While everyone's I know not where,

I'm made to sit beside him
In the sweltering semi-shade.
I yearn to run up high
To put my face up to the short-lived rain.
But if I leave, he might again
Try going somewhere on his own.
And lose his way. Or fall.

Then after muggy days and airless nights
Our ship starts trembling on its way.
On shore the silent people crowd to watch us go.
And soon it's almost night.
And through our open porthole
The distant lights grow very small,
And then are gone.
A little breeze wafts in.
Each day I meet the friendly girl again.
She speaks of foreign places, foreign names
Where St. Louis' begged for us to land,
And where they've all refused.

Yet I recall those desolated city rooms
And think that I would rather stay at sea,

Though all our meals are meagre now.
And in the bathtub all the water's salt
Instead of clear.
For after days and weeks afloat,
The briny air, the ever-changing waves,
The freedom of the open decks and passages
Have all become the kindest home I know.

I walk with shuffling Opa
On a sheltered deck.
St. Louis rocks through darkgreen northern seas.
The older girl runs up
To call us to the main deck meeting-room.
And Opa turns with us, not pausing in his prayers.
The big girl whispers in my ear:
A man has swallowed poison but will live.
And very soon we'll land.

With mother, father, and a horde of restless passengers
We wait to hear where we will go.
I hope and wish the girl will come with me.
But when we dock
Those meant for Belgium get a pretty, bright-red flower,

And so does she, and boards a waiting train.
And though I crave one too,
We're led on board a rundown freighter boat,
To bring us to some friendless, homeless port
Across another sea.

(That perfect rose I'd coveted
with all my childish hungry greed
would be my new friend's pass
to a life or death
I dare not contemplate.)

4

The Linoleum-Floored Room

When, at midnight, the St. Louis moved away from them and began her journey towards Hamburg, her home port, Lala was wide awake on the hard plank bed in the freighter's crowded hold. The other passengers pressed up the stair and through the hatch to watch the St. Louis go, and Lala went with her mother to join them. They stood on the unlit deck surrounded by the stink of engine oil, and Lala waved to the familiar, dimly seen line of stewards as they called their cheerful goodbyes across the black water. As their faces and the ship melted into silence, Lala could feel herself fading away with them. The self who remained was a seven-year-old who pressed her lips tight against fear, who walked with sober caution beside her mother's blind father, one hand poised to touch his arm when he might trip at a step or bump into a wall. This was the child who had seen the spurted blood of a suicide, who moved through her days with a hollow chest and an undiminished hunger for her missing Oma's voice.

In the dreamlike interval of the freighter's rough pitching and ploughing from the French port towards England, Lala's mind closed over much that had passed before. In her memory it is now a deep, grey, uninterrupted expanse, like a dead winter sea without waves or wind.

When they land it is morning, their first steps feel the earth sway underfoot. There are men at long wooden tables speaking foreign sounds, opening, closing trunks and cases. Blind Opa rests his hand on her shoulder, not heavily, yet still its touch makes both her shoulders bend. And then to a train with prickling plush-covered seats, framed scenes on their compartment's walls, and houses, fields, streams moving smoothly past. Then a brown paper bag and cheese sandwiches with a peculiar vinegary sweet mayonnaise inside. Her father sits leaning into the corner, studying the sandwich, silent. Her mother divides another between herself and Opa. Sometimes the train rattles and clacks beneath them and a sooty smell blows in and out of the crack at the window-top. Near the end of their journey the window suddenly turns black, as if they have entered a cave. When they slide out of it there is a green bank almost close enough to touch. Then the grey, flat, monotonous mind-sea slips back into Lala's head and she sleeps, her sandwich uneaten.

They are in one enormous room, chilly though now it's spring. The grey linoleum goes from wall to wall, marked with a murky once-yellow pattern reminding Lala of the vomit on the ship's corridor floor. One window with a thin, fly-spotted net curtain overlooks a brick wall. Between brief intervals of quiet a locomotive thunders along its length, shaking walls, curtain, the floor. Opa whispers his prayers seated on a wooden chair in the room's darkest corner. Near the window is a table covered with a once white, sour-smelling waxcloth. There are a few scratched wooden chairs. Her mother is hanging their clothes on the hooks along a wall. Several ramshackle folding-beds stand along another wall.

Someone knocks on their door and enters, bringing a warm meal in a cardboard box. Lala recognizes it is being offered with gestures of condescending pity. No conversation is possible with the English-speaking visitor, who wears a red cross on her sleeve and quickly departs again.

There is a drawer with steel cutlery and a small open cupboard with plates and mismatched cups. When they sit down to eat her father holds out his knife for her mother to see the food encrusted along its blade. Her mother gathers it all up and Lala watches her use a piece of soap, a stained dishtowel, and cold water to scrub each one. She sends Lala to fetch a clean hand towel from a suitcase in the comer with which to dry them.

Opa mutters a lowvoiced blessing. By now the food is cold. Lala eats the bits of potato which taste agreeably like the ones she used to bring to their yard dog at home – sampling a few nibbles on the way. There is a thick greenish paste which her mother says must be peas, but Lala gags when she tries to swallow it. She cannot bring herself to touch the grey slice of fish with pointed bones showing here and there. No-one notices because just then another train is surging past, and father glares with rage or fear, Lala cannot tell which, as the noise reverberates through the room, rattling the windowglass, the cups on the shelves. She has to go to the toilet and mother shows her the small windowless stall on the landing. There is no toilet paper, only some pieces of newspaper on a nail, like in the outhouse beside the stable at home.

When she comes back she is told to finish her meal. She sits and toys with the fish, lifts a few shreds to her lips, shudders and puts down her fork. Her father raises his voice over the oncoming noise of another train and orders her to finish what is on her plate. Lala tries, but a dry retching begins in her throat and it clenches shut. Her father tells her either to eat or get into her bed. Lala sits, head bowed over her plate.

Her mother pushes one of the beds away from the others, up close against a wall. It has sheets, a pillow, and one grey blanket. The sheet is wrinkled and unclean. Tears of misery and bitterness are trickling down Lala's face as she pulls off her clothes and climbs into the lumpy bed. The sheets feel damp. She sobs for a long time before falling asleep. But wakes again and again as the trains continue through the night.

⁓

In the morning a gleam of sunlight struggles through the grimy window. Everyone is dressed and talking when someone knocks at the door. In comes a woman who can speak a little of their language, though with a strong accent. She has brought eggs, bread, butter, cheese, a bottle of milk, a pretty little tin of tea, and a pot of orange marmalade, which Lala had tasted for the first time on the St. Louis. There is also a box of washing powder. She gives them some copper-coloured coins, demonstrating how to use them for hot water and heat. Then she places a wad of paper money on the table and smiles at Lala. She tells them she has been sent with these things by a Jewish charity and that someone who speaks a better German will soon come to offer them advice. She smiles again at Lala and manages to convey that she wants to show her and her mother or father the way to the school she is to attend the next day.

Her mother says she must stay behind to wash some of their things with the new soap powder. Lala and her father accompany the visitor down the steep stone steps to the street. Lala is relieved that no buses or cars are rushing by, but all the brick houses are tightly crammed on both sides of the street, without even a touch of colour in a shutter or a reminder of trees on timbered faces, like on the houses at home. And all at once, as she thinks of her village, she realizes she no longer has a home anywhere.

They walk in silence. Lala understands she is supposed to learn the way and tries to count the lampposts they are passing, but there are more and more of them, and when they turn onto another street just like theirs she loses count and stops trying. Her father stares around with a worried frown; he does not hold her hand. She hopes that later the woman will take them back to their house; she does not want to walk alone with him as he is now.

The school is a low, red brick building encircled by asphalt and a high brick wall. The woman tries to explain to her father about a piece of paper Lala will have to bring to this school, but he is hardly listening. Lala forces herself to follow what is being said, though her brain teems with the hundreds of things forcing their way in. She tries hard to guess at the meanings of the English words the woman mixes in with her faltering German.

When they pass through the school doors into the hall, there is very little light and it is very quiet. They pass closed classroom doors, and Lala hears a woman speaking loudly behind one, followed at once by the sound of children's chanting voices, which suddenly stops again. They enter a room where a woman sits writing in a book behind a wide desk. Their helper seems to be explaining about Lala beginning school. The seated woman raises questioning eyebrows at her father who remains standing in the doorway. Lala can see he is afraid and, without knowing why, becomes fearful herself. But then the woman turns and smiles at Lala with a wide smile. She rises, tells them her name, and crosses to her father, extending her hand. He hesitates, then shakes it. A bell clangs urgently just beyond the door and her father's eyes snap wide in shock. The woman says something in a soothing voice, just as there are sounds of doors opening and children's footsteps walking swiftly past in the corridor. In a moment Lala can hear their voices calling and laughing in the playground beyond the window.

Her father is asked to come to the desk and write in a book. She hears him pronounce her unaccustomed full name,

"Ursula," which sounds ugly to her ears, and no less strange than the language the two women are speaking to each other. When they are shown out again there are open classroom doors where she catches sight of close rows of empty desks and seats.

Their helper takes Lala's hand and they return to the street. At the next corner she stops, points to a sign on the railing, telling Lala to commit it to memory, so that she can find her way to school by herself. But its words are as mysterious as the Hebrew of their family's prayer books, much of which she has learned to pronounce, but without understanding. Lala does not know how to tell her this. Her father walks beside them enclosed in a daunting silence that discourages conversation. After turning several corners they reach a house which to Lala looks no different from the others, but here their helper stops. She starts to ask her father a question but falls silent when he does not look at her. Then she tells them goodbye, and wishes Lala a happy first day at school. She uses the name Ursula.

Lala begins to climb up the front steps, her father following silently behind. It is a little less chilly in their room because a slight warmth is drifting from the small gas stove. Sheets are draped over the backs of chairs in front of it, and daylight is coming unobstructed through the clean window, its curtain now removed. There is a sharpsweet soap powder smell and Lala sees there are things soaking in the sink. The waxcloth on the table emits its own thick, wet smell. Her mother's hair is covered tightly with her St. Louis scarf, and she is crouching, sweeping the floor with a handleless scrubbing brush. For a moment Lala feels relief at these signs of near-normalcy, but then she hears another train approaching fast, its thundering fills the room, and everything starts to rattle and shake as before. Even when it has receded, its memory goes on jarring the cups and plates and windowpane.

Lala has her evening meal early, so that she can go to sleep and be up in time for school the next morning. The meal of scrambled eggs and potatoes is hot, and there is warm milk in a pretty, chipped cup. Its decoration of roses with a few gold leaves Lala finds beautiful, the first lovely thing she has seen here, offering a first small hint of consolation.

It is not yet dark. The bedsheets are dry but they carry a kitchen smell of food which keeps Lala awake just as much as the din of the trains. She turns and turns but there is no escape. She calls up the pale and deep pinks of the roses on the teacup and counts them one by one, but still she cannot sleep. Then, at last the declining daylight begins to turn grey. Opa says a prayer out loud and then, through part-open lids, she sees they are eating their dinner. At its end Opa speaks a blessing before they rise. Now her mother is clearing the sink and begins to wash the dishes. Her father paces round the room. Opa is whispering his own private prayers in his chair near her bed. Lala feels a small but growing terror as she lies unsleeping, foreseeing the streets, the rows of houses, the inscrutable signs, the anonymous corners to be navigated to reach the school. And then the classroom doors, and no-one to tell her where to go in words that she can understand. Underneath her breath she begins to sob, trying not to be heard. But suddenly Opa stops his prayers. He brings his chair very close beside her, and she catches a trace of his shaving lather, and the leather smell of the prayer-thong on his arm. "Will you go to sleep, Lala, if I tell you a story?" he says very near her ear so that the oncoming train will not drown him out. When Lala nods he begins without preamble: "Once upon a time there were two children, a brother and a sister, who lived in a little house in a wood ..." And though she knows this story will soon contain terrible things, and she has not been able to forget the dream of her Oma, forever lost in this very same wood, she is soothed enough to stop sobbing. And then, even before the story has reached its end, she is asleep.

It is morning; sunlight lies on the wax tablecloth, and she smells hot cocoa, the sweet brown smell of the morning kitchen at home. On a plate are beige slices of bread spread with butter and marmalade. Her mother has put a cheese sandwich in a paper bag to bring to school. She has written the name of their street and their house number on a scrap of paper and put it in Lala's pocket. Her father is sitting on the edge of his made-up bed, cleaning and trimming his already clean and short nails with a little scissors from the nail-set they had bought in the St. Louis shop.

Her mother takes longer than usual to comb Lala's wavy hair. Someone had brought a dress for her to wear to school but now they find it is too small, and trying it on has caused knots and tangles. She has to wear the same almost outgrown dress she has worn for countless days now. Her mother goes partway down the steps with her. She asks Lala if she knows the way to school, and tells her she must first go to the head teacher she had met the day before. Lala nods, praying she will somehow find the school, though not by remembering the street signs. In some other way, perhaps like their cows who knew how to get back to the stable even after having wandered far away across the fields. But she has the new fear that when she comes back at the end of the day nobody will be there. On the bottom step she hesitates. "Will father be there when I come home?" she whispers. Her mother assures her that though they are shortly going somewhere, they will be back long before the end of school. Then she begins to climb up the stairs, sending Lala a quick wave, as if nothing unusual lay ahead.

And Lala steps onto the pavement and turns left because her body says this must be the way. But as she absorbs her new situation, filled with strangers, incomprehensible foreign words, unknown places and unforeseeable demands, a dumb, dark sense of alarm builds and spreads to a trembling sensation in her belly, just below the navel. Her heart is beating hard, too, and she casts around for somewhere pleasant to put her thoughts. She cannot find it. But then suddenly two bigger girls are coming round a corner, skipping and holding hands, who surely are also going to the school. Then several more are running to join them, and now the school's brick walls appear ahead. The girls do not go inside but begin a game in the playground. They call out to each other: Elsie! Jean! Ethel! Maureen! Lala hesitates. The school's dark green double doors seem to be locked, but then she hears a bolt being drawn and one of the doors is pushed wide open from inside. Still, the girls go on playing and Lala stands paralyzed on the step, her heart beating too fast. But then more children arrive who join her there, throwing curious glances her way and whispering to each other. She knows it is about her. She longs for someone to speak to her, to tell her what she is supposed to do next, whether to wait or go inside to find the teacher with the big desk. But now a great crowd of children is arriving, a loud bell starts its clamour, and everyone is stampeding up the steps. Until suddenly the children stop and fall silent. Lala recognizes the big desk's teacher in the doorway; she is saying something in a stern voice, and the children file silently past her into the school.

She turns her gaze on Lala, who is lingering, uncertain and apprehensive partway up the steps. The teacher smiles a large-toothed smile, motions Lala inside, and says something ending with "Ursula." Lala cringes at the unfamiliar sound of the U, which is like the start of a burp. But she nods, at a loss for how to say she is not Ursula but Lala. The teacher asks her a question of which she only understands the word, "paper." It sounds so much like the German "Papier" that Lala nods again, finds the scrap of paper with her address on it,

95

and holds it out. She takes it, glances at it, sighs, and hands it back. Then she takes Lala by the hand and brings her to a classroom with children already seated at their desks. Lala sees no other teacher there. The teacher asks the class a question. Hands shoot up and wave wildly, and all eyes stare inquisitively at Lala. The teacher calls out, "Beryl!" and a small girl with short, straight brown hair walks smiling towards them. The teacher speaks to her at some length, until Beryl solemnly says, "Yes, Miss." She takes Lala's hand and brings her to the empty desk behind her own. And Lala sits down with an overpowering sense of relief, though very close to tears. The teacher briefly addresses the class as a few last children slip into the remaining empty desks. Beryl, seated now, turns to Lala, pointing to a wooden box on her own desk, filled with bits of coloured chalk. There is a slate on which she had begun to draw. She leans close to Lala to inspect a little shelf under the desk and pulls out a slate for her. There are no chalks, however, and Beryl holds out her own, motioning Lala to take some for herself. The chalky tints are beautiful and she knows exactly what she wants to draw: a field with a rushing stream, with cows, and red and blue flowers in the grass. She is enraptured at this possibility of reinhabiting her lost home, and soon is entirely absorbed. After a few minutes Beryl leans over again and breathes a sound like "Coo!" The girl behind Lala cranes forward to see, and they whisper excitedly across her to each other. She can tell they are admiring her picture, and for a fleeting moment it seems as if there might be a place for her in this bewildering world. There is a sudden commotion as their own teacher hurriedly enters the room, and the class rises to chant a greeting. Lala quickly stumbles to her feet, head lowered to conceal her ignorant silence.

Their work begins in earnest now. Words to be learned appear on the blackboard, children read aloud from little books, and next there are rows of numbers which everyone must copy down. Lala is frozen with anxiety, but the late-arriving teacher is flustered and unaware of her problematic presence. Lala tries to look inconspicuous, studying the meaningless pages of a book from the shelf in her desk.

When a wooden crate with small bottles of cardboard-capped milk is delivered to the front of the room, the teacher chooses two children to distribute them. Lala watches everyone open theirs and begin to drink. She does the same, but the ice-cold milk is thin as water, not in the least like the thick, still-warm milk from their own cows. But she is very thirsty and drinks it all. Yet now her bladder calls for release, and no one has told her where the toilet is or if, in fact, there is one. She presses her knees together and resolves to hold it in until she gets back to their room.

A little later they all go out to the playground where everyone plays games, skips, or is clustered in groups of two or three, chattering, laughing. Lala looks round for Beryl but she has disappeared. No one approaches her or tries to speak to her. The sensation in her bladder has grown from a tiny reminder to a piercing command, against which she tightly crosses her legs and tries to shut her mind. When everyone lines up to return inside her entire concentration is bent on this effort.

Back at their desks everyone sits very still while the teacher reads aloud from a book. When she stops, the children have to answer her questions. Then they are told to tidy their desks and to stand. Now, with solemn faces everyone is singing. Lala stands with them in silence until the song reaches its last, drawn-out notes, and she realizes the class is being dismissed. She follows as everyone crowds towards the hall.

It is only as they pass through the school's outer doors and disperse onto the street that she remembers she has to find her own way home. She turns to the right and begins to walk, searching for a familiar-looking house, or iron railing, or lamppost, but they are all the same. She wavers and slows her steps, no longer sure she has chosen the right direction. Then she hears voices approaching from behind, and turns to see Beryl and another girl waving to her. They catch her up and seem to be asking where she lives. She shows them her mother's scrap of paper, and they read aloud, "Forty-four Broadhurst Gardens." With a concerned expression Beryl points to the corner ahead and they all start towards it. When they get there Beryl points to where this street meets another and mimes a turn-right gesture. Then the two girls run back the way they had come. Once there, she walks slowly, slowly, looking up at each house door. She sees the house numbers above their squares of glass and tries to match them to those on the scrap of paper. Her heart starts hammering again. What if she will not find it? But a few houses along she sees a blue enamel sign with the matching numbers. As quickly as she can she climbs the stairs to reach the longed-for toilet on the landing.

When she comes out and approaches their door she hears agitated, arguing voices – her mother's and father's – an unsettling thing which has not happened before. But then her memory recalls a long forgotten moment when her father, in irritation at her mother, had raised his voice to berate her, and Oma, who she only now realizes was *his* mother, silenced him with a quelling stare. She listens to their excited voices and then her father is shouting that this is not the time for strict dietary rules. That she should prepare the unkosher meat they have been given, that he is hungry and refuses to live on tasteless bread and cheese and scraps of stale fish. Her mother sounds beside herself and spits back how had he managed, then, in Dachau? And Lala is horror-struck at this mention of the place where the swastikaed men had taken her father. She stands stock still as her mother appeals to Opa to explain the importance of the rules they have lived by all their lives. They fall silent as he speaks a few words too low for Lala to understand. Then all is quiet again, followed by the sound of running water, the rattle of pots, and then the sudden rumble of another train.

Slowly Lala opens the door and sees her mother bent over the plate of red meat she is cutting into small pieces. Opa is saying that in extreme circumstances it is not forbidden to eat such meat. Her mother's back looks chastened.

When Lala pauses in the doorway her father barely glances at her, but Opa asks, "Is that Lala?", his face turning towards the door with his blind smile. Her mother looks round, takes in her frightened eyes and asks her what has happened. On the very edge of tears, Lala only shakes her head, willing herself not to cry because she knows not one of them could comfort her if she did. They are powerless under some terrible spell, imprisoned in this noisy, barren room, entirely ignorant of the complicated world beyond this door, more lost even than she. Instead, she cries very quietly that night, pressing her face into the pillow, so not even Opa will hear.

On the way to school the next morning, just before that uncertain corner where panic might strike, she sees Beryl and another girl ahead waiting for her. When she reaches them they walk on together, and without having to think about it, her feet learn to remember the way.

In the interval before the first lesson they are allowed to draw again and Lala finds that a box of chalks has materialized in her desk. Quickly she lays them out: a white, a green, a blue, a yellow, and a red, and begins to cover her slate with blue and green waves. She struggles to form a ship's frothy wake, gives up, and tries to draw the St. Louis itself. But she finds she does not know how it might look from the outside. Then she remembers a toy windup boat she used to play with in the bath, and begins to make a ship with many round windows, a chimney stack, and a flagpole. She adds a red flag but leaves out the swastika. It is too terrible a thing to touch and might bring its dreadful influence right into this classroom. Beryl and the other girl again lean over to admire her picture. Beryl holds out her own slate with its row of yellow circles on green sticks. Flowers, she says, with an expression of comical despair. Then she rubs them all out and holds out her yellow chalk for Lala to draw them for her. Though she does not recognize the word 'flower,' Lala can tell what she wants. She thinks of the dandelions, daisies, and buttercups in the village field, and presses her teeth onto her lower lip, putting all her effort into drawing them. Then the girl in the desk behind taps her shoulder and shows her the red flowers she has drawn, pointing at some green scribbles beside them. With a grin and a shrug she whispers, "Leaves!" Then she holds out the slate and says, "Ursie, make them for me!"

Hardly believing this could be happening, Lala happily takes the slate and draws leaves round each red flower, embellishing the picture with a strip of pointy grasses below them. The girl grins again and says, "Ta!" She has a missing front tooth and all the rest are specked with brown, but her smile is wide and warm.

Later, in the playground, the two girls pull Lala into a line where children are taking turns at jumping over a row of large squares drawn on the asphalt with chalk. At its end there is a semi-circle. "That's heaven!" Beryl says, and warns her not to land on any lines. She thinks she understands. When Beryl says, "Ursie, it's your turn," she accepts the flat pebble to be thrown and retrieved, and jumps from square to square to heaven, as she has seen the others do.

The next morning on her way to school it begins to rain. The pavement bounces back the falling raindrops, and Lala shivers as her thick wet curls stick to her ears. She tries to avoid puddles without losing her fragile sense of direction and hurries on in a kind of stupor, brought on by the splashing drops, the street's gurgling drains, and the water plashing from every downspout. Then abruptly she is shocked from her trance. An elderly woman's voice is calling her name, "Lala! Lala!" She stares ahead searching for its source. Rain and puddles forgotten, she runs towards it and sees the open window and an old face looking down, calling to someone hurrying away along the street. "Laura! Laura! Don't forget!" The voice calls. The woman on the street waves a hand in acknowledgement before she vanishes round the next corner, and the window bangs shut.

Lala reaches the school drenched. The teacher tells them to remove their soaked shoes and socks and put them beside the warm pipe that runs along the wall. There is a furtive stirring as children waggle naked feet at each other and whisper joking insults about filthy toenails. They are allowed to draw for a little while, and Lala scrubs at her slate to remove the remains of yesterday's picture. For a long time she gazes at the black surface with its bloom of chalkdust, but no flower or tree or beast, no stream or house asks to be drawn. She touches the blue chalk to the cool slate and lets it wander till it has made a curving rising and falling line. She makes its echo just below it, and then another and another, until almost half the slate is covered. Her hand and forearm move in a slow dance, back and forth over the slate, and she sways slightly as if rocked by remembered waves.

Beryl turns round to peer and whispers, "That's pretty. What is it?" Lala stops to look at what she has drawn. Then her hand finds the leafgreen chalk to make circles, like bubbles between the curving lines. A third of the slate is still blank. She is gazing at this empty space when, for just a split second, the old woman's calling voice flashes through her memory, and she thinks how no one here calls her by her real name. Then the room's busy, rustling silence is back and she begins to form her name over and over, as carefully as if she were drawing a flower. And when there is a whole row of Lalas, she tries to remember if there is an English word – any word – she now can write. She takes the bright pink chalk and prints a whole line of ball, ball, ball, ball, ball. And then, in the remaining space, slowly and carefully, she completes a last row with the word, Oma. She inscribes it with all her attention on the chalk's tip, and tries to make each O a completely perfect circle, an unconscious talisman of safety and protection.

⤳

She can easily find her way to school and back now. Sometimes in the mornings Beryl and one or two other girls wait for her at the corner. Once, holding hands, they all skipped together, shrieking if one of them jumped on a crack. And once, on the way home, Beryl showed her a sweet shop on a nearby busy street where, with a big brown penny and some tiny coins called farthings, she bought a little paper bag of very sweet raspberry drops which she shared with Lala.

A few days later, as Lala climbs the stairs to the linoleum-floored room, she hears raised, agitated voices. The instant she touches the door handle they fall silent, but not before she has heard her father's fraught exclamation, *"Mutter,"* and with sudden anguish knows they were talking about Oma. She enters, trying to read her parents' guarded faces. Her mother is sticking a needle into a sock she is mending, and her father is pacing the room. A train begins to announce itself through the floorboards, and Opa, who is seated on his chair in the corner, directs his sightless smile towards her. She wants desperately to know what they had been saying, but it is clear she is not supposed to have heard. That to have listened at all is to have broken the never openly declared iron rule that Oma must not be spoken of, either by her or in her hearing.

The train's thunder fills the room, then roars past with its aftermath of trembling windowglass and clattering dishes. Her mother tells her she should have some bread and butter after she has washed her hands. And as the water dribbles from the tap she hears her father speak to Opa, saying a word she has not heard before: *Krieg,* war. She shuts off the water, waiting for Opa's reply, but he remains silent.

Lala asks, "What does Krieg mean?"

Her father does not stop his pacing, her mother is silent, but Opa lifts one hand to his face to touch his eyes, and says, "The Krieg was when my eyes stopped seeing." And Lala thinks he means that what he would have had to look at with seeing eyes was too terrible to bear. So she persists, asking why his eyes cannot see again now, but Opa shakes his head, tapping his fingers on his knees – his habit when he is not absorbed in praying. He seems to be weighing what he should say. But her father stops his pacing in front of Opa, who at last says, "Soon, there will be war again."

And later that evening, while sitting round the table, ready for mother to bring them the meal she has prepared, the woman from the charity who speaks a little German arrives with a letter for them from an uncle in America. Her father reads aloud that their newspapers say England will shortly be at war with Germany. As father reaches the letter's end their visitor agrees that war is only weeks away. She adds that arrangements are being made to send all of London's schoolchildren to the countryside, away from the expected bombs. The woman's quick glance at Lala tells her she, too, will be one of these children now.

And so it was. Lala, a luggage label with the name Ursula tied round her neck, and Opa's little leather suitcase in her hand, was sent away as well. Without her family now, with classmates and teachers boarding a train which carried them between green embankments, past small suburban gardens, till they came to the fields and woods of the open countryside. And then further still, in a low, green bus which brought them through the leafy, dusty, summer lanes to their unknown village homes. And to the makeshift schoolrooms in metal

huts beside the village churchyard. To lodge with strangers
in their narrow, crowded homes. To attend Sunday service in
the ancient square-towered church, which soon will shelter
them each time the siren lifts its piercing warning wail. Here
they will root, to grow like alien seeds transplanted by an
unexpected storm blowing them through woods and fields.
Most will be happy, many run wild, a handful weep for their
gritty London streets and are fetched back home, but those that
stay, survive.

Maybe it's been a year
In this small house
With Jim, the old brown cat
And quavery-voiced Miss Brown,
Who moves her thin shape awkwardly across the room,
To light the brittle mantle on the wall,
Till its bright flare lights up the food
She cooks upon the stove.
And always Jim will join us on his empty chair
To share our evening meal.

Miss Brown is kind
But says she never had a child before
To feed, to bathe, to help with clothes and bed,
And never was a child herself.
Though how she came into the world
All bony, tall, and old
She's never told.

⮑

That London room's far, far away,
But sometimes there's a postcard I can almost read.
It always ends, *Viele Grüsse und Küsse, deine Mutter.*
As if she'd always kissed me many times.
The spiky German script unlocks
Some dim-remembered shreds of dreams,
Of moonlit cobbles and the sound of father's voice.
The silky feel of Oma's braided hair
As I reach out to hold her hairpins in my hand.
And once a splash of something red and bright.
But after school where now we climb the thick-limbed trees,
Or race away in hide-and-seek

Till one of us is found and It,
These dwindling images dissolve.
I learn to know how fast my legs can carry me,
And Cockney speech comes easy to my tongue.
And here, where I am Ursie-Ursula,
I am not banished, as before,
But even once was sent as messenger
To meet and guide a London visitor
Past churchyard gate on winding graveside paths
Until we reached the metal hut that's now our school.

And though some nights I cannot stop myself
From crying at the misery in my chest,
I've come to love the patterns of my newfound days:
The prayers in words that I can understand;
The gutter marble games; the weekly comics' fierce appeal;
The sugar shocks of brightly coloured sweets;
The easy, unwatched friendships of the woods and village lanes.

I shiver when I think of what my family might say
When first they come to live here as they write they will.
Already I can hear my mother's scathing tone

About my friends, those unwashed children of the streets,
Their heedless noisy games till hours after dark.
And worst of all, my unresisting worship with Miss Brown
Inside the ancient alien church.

Then I can't keep from wondering,
If only she were here,
If Oma'd understand.
And say it's best to think of kindness first
And let me go on playing with my friends.
(Though I know even she would not allow
my Sunday presence in a church.)

So, sure of deprivations soon to come
I make my friends write down their names:
Beryl, Reenie, Margaret, and Pauline,
On bits of paper I have kept from school.
And every time we're sent to shelter in the church,
When we receive some things with which to draw –
Perhaps to take our minds off all the thumps and crumps

Of war beyond these flint and sandstone walls –
I take my pencil,
Shade in every lovely arch and span,
And then the timber rafters, dark
Against the plaster overhead.
And even every high-up corbel head of stone
Carved with a wicked face.

All this and more I slowly made my own,
Until at last it stilled the voice
That called for Oma in the night.
It filled the empty space inside my chest
That used to make me cry,
And let me walk and run and play
Like any other child.

Just yesterday at dusk,
Chanting a skipping rhyme,
We all fell quiet to hear
A flying, high up bird
Whistling its lovely endless song.
I'd heard that same song long ago,

When, one by one, our grazing cows
Began their ambling homeward path
Over the trodden grass,
Till they were back at home.
I think perhaps this was the selfsame bird
Come all that way
Like me.

Translations

PAGE 15
God's greeting
Dear God
God be thanked

PAGE 22
grape meringue tart

PAGE 24
The night was black
The moon shone bright
When on a sandbank
Lightening fast
A hare on skates
Glided slowly past.

Afterword
by Doris L. Bergen

And then I forced myself
To look in father's face,
To ask those burning questions
I'd heard no one speak.

But father would not look at me.
He turned away.
His frozen silence told me
That my dreadful dream was true,
And Oma was now lost to me.

This beautiful and surprising book tells of a Jewish girl in
Nazi Germany, her family's attempt to escape on board the
St. Louis, and the beginning of their refuge in Britain. It is a
tribute to childhood and tradition, to the tastes and sounds

of the south German countryside where the author spent her first seven years, to the people who helped her family, and to her beloved grandmother. The author offers a rare perspective on some major events and illuminates less familiar aspects of the German Jewish past. At the same time her account is a wrenching reminder of the particular vulnerability of all children, anywhere, in times of war and political upheaval.

The first part of the book depicts a pastoral idyll shattered by violence. The author's father and grandfather were cattle dealers, who owned their own home and stables. As rural people, they were a minority among the 500,000 Jews in Germany in the 1930s but they were not anomalous. Thousands of Jews lived in small towns and villages, particularly in the Rhine valley, where a Jewish presence dated back to Roman times. The small Orthodox synagogue in the author's village was one of many Jewish places of worship scattered throughout southwestern Germany. Although industrialization and urbanization in the nineteenth century had drawn many Germans, Jewish and gentile, to the rapidly growing cities, some Jews remained on the land, where they worked in agriculture, trades, and all manner of small businesses. Their cattle grazed the lush pastures of the Rhine valley; they were vintners, shoemakers, housewives, shopkeepers, and peddlers. Their lifestyle often differed little from that of the Christians around them, and most, like their neighbours, were neither wealthy nor influential.

Jews in rural Germany were affected in specific ways by the antisemitism that became institutionalized after Adolf Hitler came to power in 1933. Jewish families who had lived amidst Christians for generations found themselves increasingly isolated: in small towns and villages, everyone knew who they were. Boycotts, all manner of restrictions, and propaganda made it uncomfortable for non-Jews to associate with them and rewarded those who joined in the persecution. Gentiles who owed money to Jews suddenly found it easy not to repay those debts, to demand more credit or special deals, or simply to take what they wanted. Christians and Jews in friendly and loving relationships were targets of public humiliations and vicious attacks.

Under these conditions, between 1933 and 1939 many rural Jews left for the cities. They sought the safety of numbers and the educational, religious, and social services that the large Jewish communities of Frankfurt am Main, Munich, and Berlin could offer. Others tried to flee Germany altogether. Those Jews who stayed in the country found they were at the mercy of their neighbours. Communities dominated by even a small number of ardent Nazis became impossible for Jews, who were open targets for assault on their possessions and their bodies. Meanwhile, in villages where decent people held key positions – mayor, chief of police, priest, pastor – Jews could sometimes live relatively undisturbed, at least in the early Nazi years.

Nazi authorities instituted hundreds of laws and regulations directed at Jews in Germany. These included major pieces of legislation, most famously the Nuremberg Laws of 1935 that forbade Jews and so-called Aryans from marrying or having intimate relations and stripped Jews of the rights of German citizenship. But petty restrictions also added to the torment. By the war years, Jews could not own typewriters, radios, telephones, livestock, or pets; they could live only in designated buildings and enter shops only at particular times; trains, schools, parks, and beaches were off limits; they could not buy chocolate, eggs, shaving cream, or soap; they were forced to surrender their driving licenses, bicycles, and library cards. These measures created hardships for Jews and served Nazi propaganda purposes at the same time. Sometimes what seemed only a minor inconvenience could constitute a severe blow to Jewish life and an antisemitic propaganda coup. For example, by prohibiting Jews from purchasing or receiving cow's milk, Nazi authorities deprived Jewish children of tasty, comforting things, weakened their health, and reinforced the stereotype of Jews as unwholesome, dangerous, and even demonic. Meanwhile, with consumer goods scarce, the ban on milk also sent the message to non-Jewish Germans that shortages or high prices were not due to poor planning or military spending but were somehow caused by Jewish greed.

Taken together such restrictions produced what has been called the "social death" of German Jews. As economic, social, and even familial ties between Jews and the rest of the population were severed, Jews became pariahs in their own country. Non-Jews did not need to be fanatical antisemites in order to contribute to this destructive dynamic: they only needed to obey the law and follow their self-interest.

The author and her family left Germany in 1939, only months before the war began and before the full force of the Nazi onslaught against Jews. Still, her account shows the ravages of social death and her vantage point as a child gives particular insight into how the system functioned. Children were often the first to feel the sting of public prejudice. Unlike many of their mothers, they interacted with non-Jews regularly and constantly, in school and on the way there and back. Unlike their fathers, they lacked professional standing, resources, and contacts that could provide some buffer from abuse. Schoolyard bullies and mean, antisemitic, or simply ambitious teachers could do whatever they wanted to Jewish children, knowing they were backed by official ideology and policy. Teachers set the tone for their pupils. When the author's teacher banished Jewish and Romani children to a bench at the back of the room and permitted children to watch out the window as men they knew, perhaps their own fathers, beat their Jewish neighbours, it is not surprising that her classmates taunted her and threw stones.

There are few published accounts to tell us more about what the Romani boys the author mentions experienced. We do know that the first major round-ups and incarceration of Romani in Nazi Germany had already come in 1936 and that by 1945 at least one quarter of a million Romani people had been murdered by Nazi Germans and collaborators all over Europe. There is no documented evidence of efforts by "ordinary Germans" to aid Romani victims of persecution.

Elderly Jews also suffered in particular ways during the time of "social death." Jews desperate to flee Germany often found it impossible or prohibitively expensive to get visas for older family members, who were not valued as labour. Some people left parents and grandparents behind; others missed opportunities to escape in order to keep their families together. Between 1933 and 1938, the suicide rate among older Jews in Germany skyrocketed.

As a Jewish child from a farming village, the author has a rare and valuable view of the Kristallnacht pogrom of November 1938. Kristallnacht, often referred to as the "night of broken glass," is usually associated with shattered store windows and the burning of hundreds of synagogues across Germany, annexed Austria, and the Sudetenland. Here we see other forms of destruction. Police arrested the author's father, as they did 26,000 other Jewish men, and sent him to the Dachau concentration camp. Villagers smashed into the family's home, stealing and demolishing their possessions. Such personalized violence was typical of the Kristallnacht in rural areas. Local Nazi Party members and Stormtroopers received their orders by telephone down the chain of command from Berlin. In some cases they misunderstood instructions, in others they seized the opportunity to settle old scores. Many of the Jews murdered during the Kristallnacht were killed in small-town actions of this sort.

Through the author's eyes, we see how the Kristallnacht devastated not only property but families. The author describes her mother's frenzy to gather the money needed to free her father and buy the family's way out of Germany. In late 1938, thousands of Jewish women were trying to do the same thing: selling gold, jewelry, and possessions of all kinds for whatever they could get; waiting at consulates and embassies in the hope of obtaining visas; using every charm, connection, and resource they could muster to try to get their men released. But the author also reveals something rarely discussed: the effect of those days, weeks, and in some cases months in concentration camps on German Jewish men. Her father emerged unrecognizable to her, distant and broken. Camp authorities made prisoners they released vow never to speak of what they had suffered, but through the eyes of a bewildered child we see another kind of crushing silence.

In May 1939, the *St. Louis*, a German transatlantic liner, set sail from Hamburg to Havana. On board were almost one thousand passengers, the overwhelming majority Jewish and all but one of them refugees. Among them were the author, her parents, and her grandfather. When the ship arrived, Cuban authorities refused to allow the passengers to disembark. Some of their visas had been issued against the orders of the Cuban government by a diplomat who enriched himself in the process, and there was vociferous opposition within Cuba to allowing in more Jewish refugees. For days the ship remained offshore while representatives of the passengers tried to negotiate with the Cubans or find some alternative destination. Finally the *St. Louis* left Havana. Sailing slowly up the coast of Florida and then northward, its captain radioed officials all along the way in the United States and Canada, but no one would permit the ship to dock.

After weeks at sea, the ship returned to Europe. Its deliberately protracted route bought Jewish organizations time to arrange refuge for all of the passengers in Britain, France, Belgium, and the Netherlands. The captain, Gustav Schroeder, did what he could to facilitate negotiations and to ensure that his crew treated their passengers as they would any others. In 1993, he was posthumously recognized by Yad Vashem in Israel as Righteous Among the Nations, a gentile who risked his well-being to help save Jews. Of the *St. Louis* passengers who, like the author, ended up in Britain, all but one, who died in an air raid, survived the war. Half of those who returned to the continent were killed in the Holocaust.

The author arrived in England with her parents and grandfather, four of the German Jews who managed to enter the United Kingdom before Germany invaded Poland in September 1939. By then, over half the Jews of Germany had fled. Desperate parents dispatched thousands of unaccompanied Jewish children to England with the Kindertransport. Of those Jews left behind in Germany, only a few thousand survived, almost all of them adults who were married to non-Jews.

The book ends with another separation, through the British evacuation scheme known as Operation Pied Piper. Perhaps that fanciful code-name appealed to a girl who dreamed in fairy tales. In the first days of the war, almost three million people, most of them schoolchildren, were removed from London and other urban centres to the English countryside as experts expected massive German air-raids that would flatten Britain's cities and kill millions of people. Although the death toll was less catastrophic than feared, many British children experienced evacuation as a trauma of homesickness and loss. For the author, however, it was the beginning of a return to life.

Suggestions for Further Reading

Bergen, Doris L. *The Holocaust: A Concise History*. Lanham, MD: Rowman and Littlefield, 2009.

Dwork, Debórah, and Robert Jan van Pelt. *Flight from the Reich: Refugee Jews, 1933–1946*. New York: W.W. Norton, 2009.

Engelmann, Bernd. *Inside Hitler's Germany*. New York: Pantheon, 1985.

Friedländer, Saul. *Nazi Germany and the Jews*, vol. 1, *The Years of Persecution*. New York: HarperCollins, 1997.

Fritzsche, Peter. *Life and Death in the Third Reich*. Cambridge, MA: Harvard University Press, 2008.

Goeschel, Christian. *Suicide in Nazi Germany*. New York: Oxford University Press, 2009.

Jones, Elizabeth B. *Gender and Rural Modernity: Farm Women and the Politics of Labor in Germany, 1871–1933*. Farnham: Ashgate, 2009.

Kaplan, Marion A. *Between Dignity and Despair: Jewish Life in Nazi Germany*. New York: Oxford University Press, 1998.

Klemperer, Victor. *I Will Bear Witness: A Diary of the Nazi Years, 1933–1941*. New York: Random House, 1998.

London, Louise. *Whitehall and the Jews, 1933–1948: British Immigration Policy, Jewish Refugees and the Holocaust*. New York: Cambridge University Press, 2000.

Miller, Scott, and Sarah A. Ogilvie. *Refuge Denied: The* St. Louis *Passengers and the Holocaust*. Madison, WI: University of Wisconsin Press, 2006.

Rosenberg, Otto. *A Gypsy in Auschwitz*. London: London House, 1999.

Steinweis, Alan E. *Kristallnacht 1938*. Cambridge, MA: Harvard University Press, 2009.

Stephenson, Jill. *Hitler's Home Front: Württemberg under the Nazis*. New York: Hambledon Continuum, 2006.